Exercises in
African-American Funk
Mangambe, Bikutsi, and the Shuffle

by Jonathan Joseph
and Steve Rucker

Design and layout by Scott Bienstock

Photos by Mike Jachles

Published by:
Modern Drummer Publications, Inc.
271 Route 46 West
Suite H-212
Fairfield, NJ 07004 USA

CONTENTS

Foreword

The purpose of this book is to introduce musicians who have studied jazz, R&B, rock, soul, and blues to a concept that applies West African rhythms to various genres. The information is presented from my perspective as a jazz drummer who has studied many styles of music over the past forty years.

My fascination with the marriage of African and American musical cultures began in the late 1990s, while I was living in New York City and met Cameroonian bassist Richard Bona. We quickly became friends and played various gigs together, resulting in my becoming a member of Bona's band for two years. I had previously worked with jazz/world fusion keyboardist Josef Zawinul, as a member of the Zawinul Syndicate, but I knew this gig with Richard would help me solidify even further some of the concepts I had been working on. Through the process of learning Richard's original material, and performing the music of Weather Report and Jaco Pastorius as a part of the set, my perception of rhythm and time was transformed. I was introduced to a rhythmic concept of which I had no prior knowledge. (It was certainly beyond my understanding of Afro-Cuban 6/8 rhythms.) I found that it was difficult to locate the first beat of each measure, which made it very challenging to play Richard's music.

Bona explained the rhythms to me from his perspective as a native African. Intellectually, this was a struggle. As an American musician, I had grown up with certain concepts, and I had developed a mindset that was firmly rooted in American culture. In order to incorporate these African concepts into my playing, I had to translate the information into a language that I could understand. The results are what's included in this book. Hope you enjoy it!

—**Jonathan Joseph**

Introduction

The series of exercises contained in this book will guide you through a fusion of African and American elements. On the American side, we have shuffle and shuffle-funk. On the African side, we have the rhythms from Cameroon known as mangambe and bikutsi. Playing these exercises will strengthen your groove, provide you with an understanding of the three-against-four polyrhythm, give you an awareness of the second partial of the triplet, and introduce you to a fresh new way to hear and feel music.

Syncopation and Independence

Having a clear understanding of syncopation and independence is essential to enabling you to play the complete patterns with the correct feel. Throughout the book, we'll look at each of these elements and examine how they work together. After mastering the exercises, you will be able to hear both sides of the three-against-four polyrhythm at the same time. It'll take patience and persistence to master all of the concepts that will be presented, but the payoff will be worth the effort.

The examples begin by presenting the rhythms in their most basic forms. We will then add elements with subsequent exercises. Some of the exercises may be frustrating at first, but stay with it. Having an effective system of practice will minimize the frustration you experience while developing your independence. We recommend practicing each exercise for a maximum of twenty minutes. Once you've worked on one idea for the allotted time, move on to practice something that's not related to polyrhythms. We've found this to be the most effective way to internalize challenging material. The distraction of practicing a new, unrelated idea allows your subconscious to process the rhythm and independence of the exercises. After stepping away for about twenty minutes, try the challenging exercise again. Repeat the process until you've mastered it. Try this method as you work through the book, as well as with any new material you may be studying.

Using a Metronome

Practicing with a metronome is essential to developing a stable and consistent time feel. When using a metronome, it's important to have a positive attitude toward it. The metronome should be viewed as a friend, which makes it easier for you to play a groove with good time. The nature of the three-against-four polyrhythm is that each element of the rhythm has its own meter, so you can modulate to either one relative to the original pulse.

Having the consistent pulse of the metronome will help you strengthen your internal clock. Once you're comfortable with the independence and syncopation aspects of the exercises as they relate to the pulse of the metronome, you'll need to learn to ignore the metronome—while at the same time being aware of it—in order to achieve the proper feel. Once you can hear both vantage points of the rhythm, you will be able to change the feel of what you're playing without dropping a beat. And you will be well on your way to learning the joys of African-American funk!

Notation Key

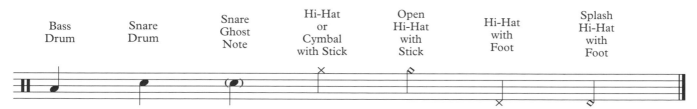

| Bass Drum | Snare Drum | Snare Ghost Note | Hi-Hat or Cymbal with Stick | Open Hi-Hat with Stick | Hi-Hat with Foot | Splash Hi-Hat with Foot |

Acknowledgments

"I would like to thank God for blessing me with the gift of the music, along with my wife, Wendy Joseph, and my mother, Jerlen Joseph, for their unending love and support. I would also like to thank my sponsors: Sakae, Sabian, Evans, Regal Tip, 2Box, and Drumasonic."

—**Jonathan Joseph**

"Thanks to Claudia, Bryan, and Matt for their constant love and support. Thanks as well to Remo, Sabian, Vic Firth, Rez Drums, the Frost School at the University of Miami, and the UM Drum Nation."

—**Steve Rucker**

Chapter 1: Three-Against-Four Polyrhythm

The first thing we need to address is the three-against-four polyrhythm, which is crucial to many African rhythms. It's necessary for you to be able to hear and feel this rhythm in order to apply some of the concepts presented later. In the exercises, hearing the rhythm is as important as, if not more important than, actually playing the patterns.

Let's learn to hear the three-against-four polyrhythm. Play the following triplet exercise on the hi-hat. Be sure to use a metronome or external sound source. Start at a tempo of 80 bpm. As you're playing this exercise, keep the tempo steady and count out loud: "One, two, three, four."

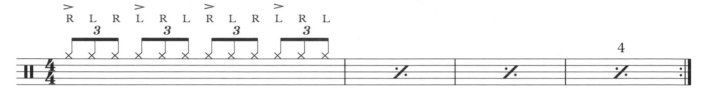

Now change the pattern so that you're accenting every fourth triplet partial. Count those accents out loud as "One, two, three." Technically, the polyrhythm is 3:4. For the purpose of this book, we will refer to this rhythm as the "long three," because of the way the pattern feels relative to the quarter-note pulse in 4/4.

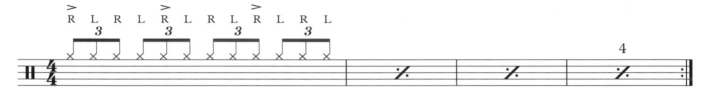

It might help to ground this rhythm with the bass drum.

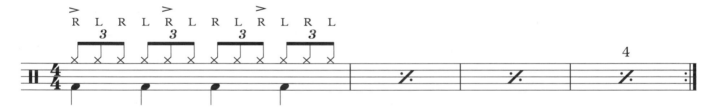

It's important to remember that this is an exercise for the mind. The space between the triplet partials never changes—the only thing that shifts is your perception of the accents against the metronome.

When you can really hear the polyrhythm, alternate between two measures of 4/4 and two measures of the long three. As you're playing the exercise, keep the tempo steady and count out loud "One, two, three, four" with the accents in bars 1 and 2, and count "One, two, three" with the accents in bars 3 and 4.

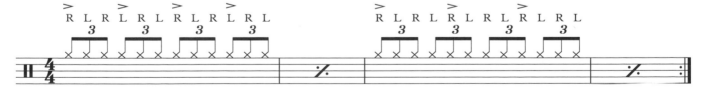

Here's the same exercise with quarter notes on the bass drum.

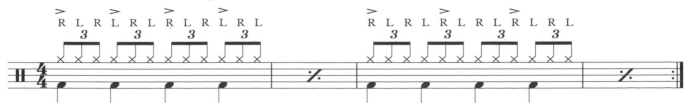

To make it more interesting and fun, play the previous exercise along with recordings that have a triplet subdivision, such as "Babylon Sisters" by Steely Dan.

Now play the bass drum on the accented notes.

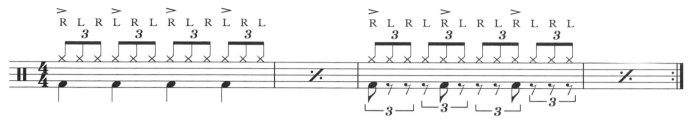

Now play the same exercise with triplets on the ride cymbal.

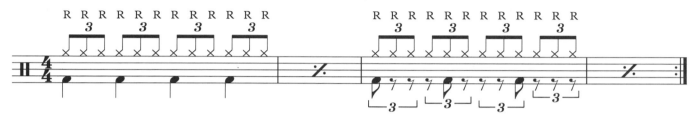

Now play the bass drum rhythm from the last exercise with the hi-hat foot.

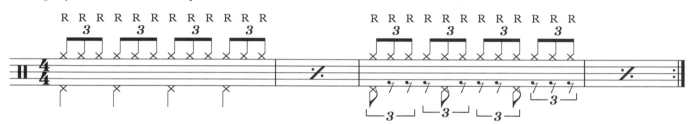

In this next exercise, play quarter notes on the bass drum for two measures, then play the long three with the hi-hat foot for two measures.

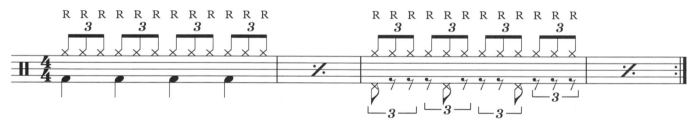

The next step is to play quarter notes and the long three at the same time. Start by playing quarter notes on the bass drum.

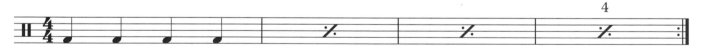

Then add the hi-hat foot on beat 1 while singing the 8th-note triplets out loud.

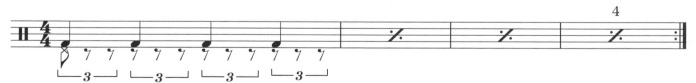

Next, add a hi-hat note on the second partial of the triplet on beat 2. First sing the rhythm, and then play it.

When that feels comfortable, add a third hi-hat note on the third triplet partial on beat 3. Now our polyrhythm is complete!

The musicality of this exercise should be apparent by the time you get to the complete polyrhythm. You may be tempted to alter the sonic placement of the long three, such as by playing it with your left hand on the snare. While that is a valid way of expressing the polyrhythm, it's important to realize that this is an independence exercise designed to give you the skills you'll need to combine the African and American elements found later in the book. We encourage you to develop the exercises as they are presented, in order to master these very important concepts.

Next, add triplets on the ride cymbal to the previous exercise.

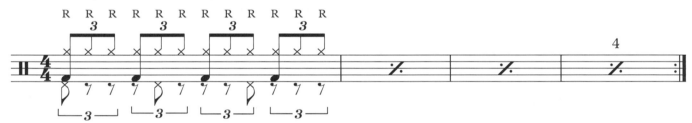

Here's the pattern with the feet written a different way.

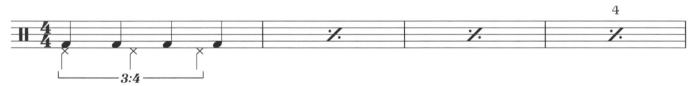

Using this notation, you can clearly see the 4/4 and 3/4 meters stacked on top of one another.

For the next exercise, use your muscle memory to keep the rhythm steady, and focus on hearing the hi-hat pattern as quarter notes in 3/4 and the bass drum as a counter-rhythm in 4/4. When you're hearing the rhythm in 3/4, the bass drum will sound like the following.

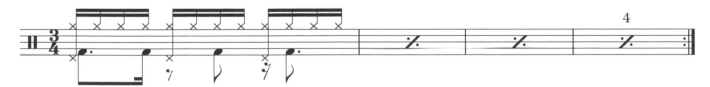

It might be easier for you to hear the polyrhythm in 3/4 if you play the snare on beats 2 and 3. As you're doing that, count out loud: "One, two, three."

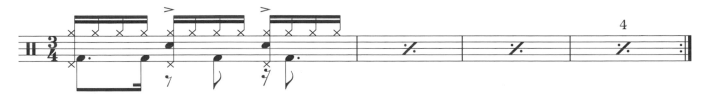

Now alternate between these next two exercises. Make sure that the time is steady and the rhythm stays exactly the same when you switch meters. The only thing that's changing is the way you're hearing the rhythm. To anyone listening, it will sound as though you're playing the same thing over and over.

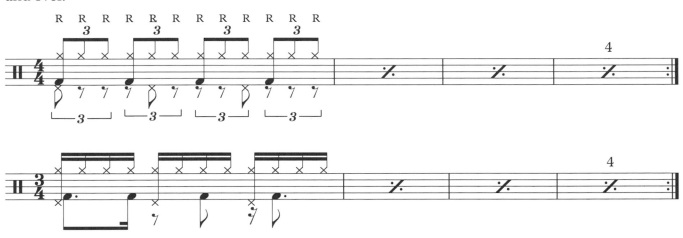

Chapter 2: Six-Against-Four Polyrhythm

The next step in our exploration of African polyrhythms is to learn to hear and play six against four. This polyrhythm is very prevalent in West African music, and there's a direct relationship between it and the long three, as you'll see.

This is the basic six-against-four polyrhythm. The upper rhythm consists of quarter notes in 4/4 meter, and the lower rhythm is quarters in 6/4.

This is the same rhythm written a different way. Here, the lower rhythm is written as quarter-note triplets.

Still another way of notating this polyrhythm is to write the lower rhythm as 8th-note triplets with every other note being played.

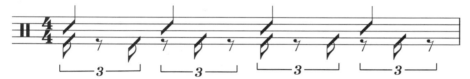

Now we'll apply the method that we used for hearing the long three from Chapter 1. Play the following triplet exercise on the hi-hat. Use a metronome to keep the tempo steady, and count out loud: "One, two, three, four."

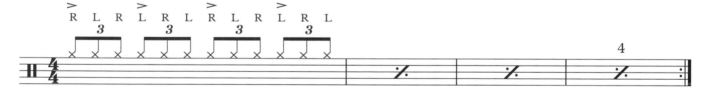

Now change the accents so that you're playing every other triplet partial. Count out loud: "One, two, three, four, five, six." You don't have to play this exercise on a drumset, and some of you may find the rhythm easier to hear than the long-three exercises in Chapter 1.

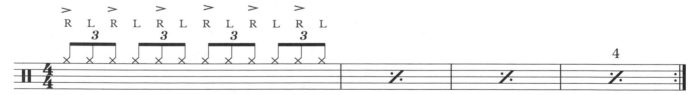

Next, alternate between two measures of 4/4 and two measures of six against four. As you're playing this exercise, keep the tempo steady and count out loud "One, two, three, four" with the accents in bars 1 and 2, and "One, two, three, four, five, six" with the accents in bars 3 and 4. Again, to make the exercise more interesting and fun, play it along with some recordings that have a triplet subdivision.

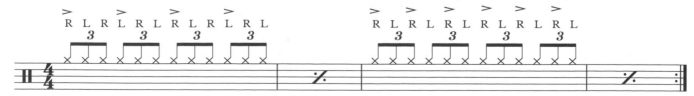

Now play the bass drum on the accented notes.

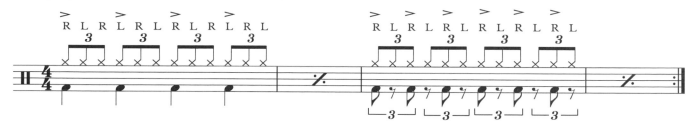

Now play the same exercise with triplets on the ride cymbal.

Here's the same exercise played with the hi-hat foot.

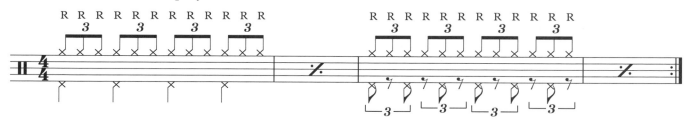

In the next exercise, play quarter notes with the bass drum for two measures, and then play six against four with the hi-hat foot for two measures.

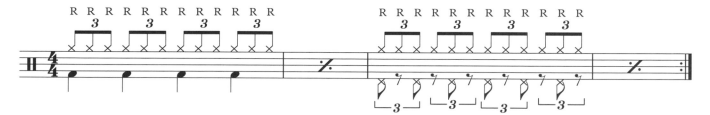

The next step is to play quarter notes and six against four at the same time. Start by playing quarter notes with the bass drum.

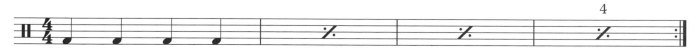

Now add the hi-hat foot on beat 1, while singing 8th-note triplets.

Next, add the hi-hat notes one at a time until the six-against-four polyrhythm is complete.

Now add triplets on the ride cymbal.

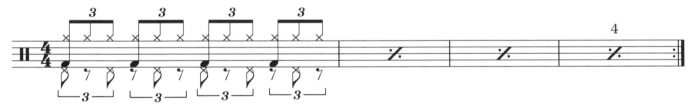

From here, feel free to experiment with cymbal variations, and, if you wish, add the snare drum on beats 2 and 4 of the bar or on beat 3. We will explore many more drumset grooves using this six-against-four polyrhythm in upcoming chapters.

Chapter 3: American Shuffle

In this chapter, we're taking a look at some basic American shuffle grooves. As with many of the exercises in this book, we'll begin with a groove to be played with the hands. Then we'll offer a list of bass drum options.

When you practice these grooves, a strong sense of time is paramount. As mentioned in the introduction, it's important to practice with a metronome. This will show you what your tendencies are at various tempos. You can also use a different external sound source, such as a sequencer or audio track, provided its timing is solid.

All of the grooves in this chapter have the traditional shuffle pattern, which can be played on the hi-hat or the ride cymbal. The snare is played on beats 2 and 4, which is often referred to as the "backbeat." We're starting with these basic shuffle grooves to begin your journey into the triplet world.

Ghost notes are introduced on the snare in hand patterns 2 and 3. These notes should be played as softly as possible and should be felt by the listener more than heard. The best way to achieve this sound is to keep the stick very close to the drumhead. The backbeats should be played from a much greater stick height.

It can be helpful in the course of practicing to alternate between a very simple shuffle groove and the more challenging patterns included here. For example, you could play four bars of a simple shuffle followed by four bars of the exercise. This process causes you to move into and out of your comfort zone.

Probably the most common drumset shuffle is the following. This groove has been used for many years in blues music. It's the ideal representation of the "American" component of this book. Traditionally, the emphasis is on the quarter-note downbeats, with a secondary emphasis on the third partial of the triplets. We can play the triplets with a tight, or closed, feel, or we can play them with a very wide and more relaxed feel.

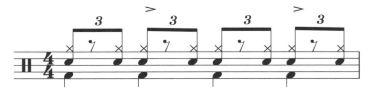

For the exercises in this chapter, we'll start with a very simple version of the shuffle and gradually add ghost notes. Play each pattern at a tempo range of 70 to 130 bpm.

Hand Pattern 1

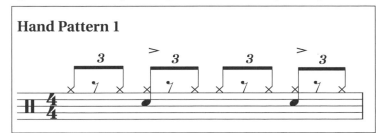

Here are some exercises that layer Hand Pattern 1 with different bass drum rhythms.

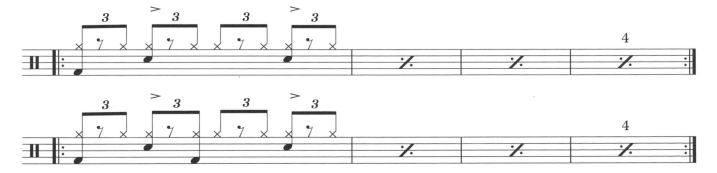

Hand Pattern 2

Here are some exercises that layer Hand Pattern 2 with different bass drum rhythms.

Hand Pattern 3

Here are some exercises that layer Hand Pattern 3 with different bass drum rhythms.

Chapter 4: Half-Time Shuffle-Funk

In this chapter, we move the backbeat of the shuffle groove over to beat 3. What this does is transform the shuffle into a half-time, triplet-based funk groove, which we'll call "shuffle-funk." The Purdie shuffle, made famous by the legendary R&B drummer Bernard Purdie, is one version of this type of groove.

The first hand pattern contains no ghost notes. The grooves become more and more dense as we add ghost notes. As in the previous exercises, the ghost notes should be played extremely soft. The primary focus of the groove is on the bass drum and the backbeat.

As mentioned before, it's very helpful in your practice to alternate between a simple groove and the more difficult exercise. For instance, you can switch between each line of the exercises and this traditional mangambe groove.

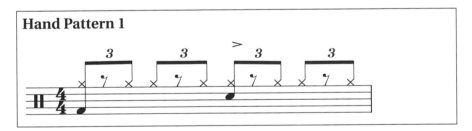

Although these exercises are written with 8th-note triplets for consistency, you might also conceptualize them as 16th-note triplets. That interpretation would put the backbeat on beats 2 and 4 of a bar of 4/4. So Hand Pattern 3 would look like the following.

As before, we'll start with a simple hand pattern and gradually add ghost notes. Practice the exercises between 70 and 130 bpm.

Hand Pattern 1

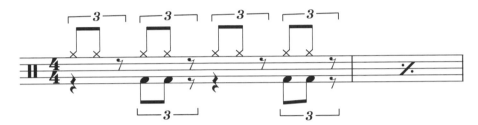

Here are some exercises that use Hand Pattern 1 with different bass drum variations.

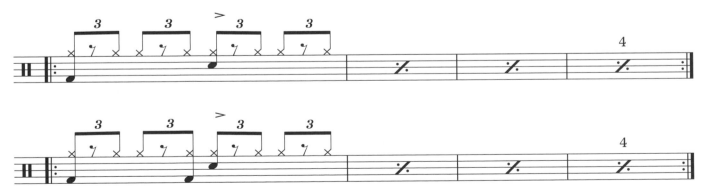

Hand Pattern 2

Here are some exercises that use Hand Pattern 2 with different bass drum variations.

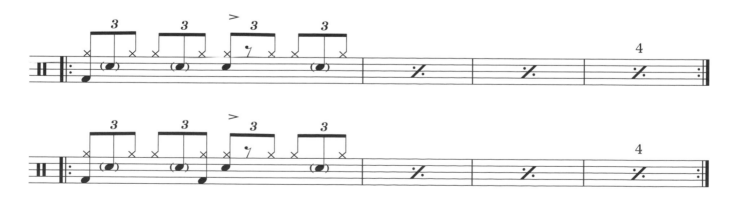

Hand Pattern 3

Here are some exercises that use Hand Pattern 3 with different bass drum variations.

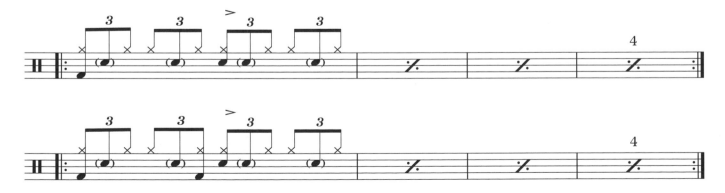

Hand Pattern 4

Here are some exercises that use Hand Pattern 4 with different bass drum variations.

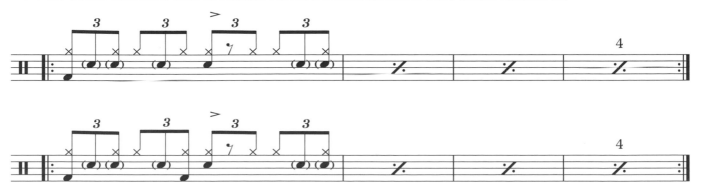

Hand Pattern 5

Here are some exercises that use Hand Pattern 5 with different bass drum variations.

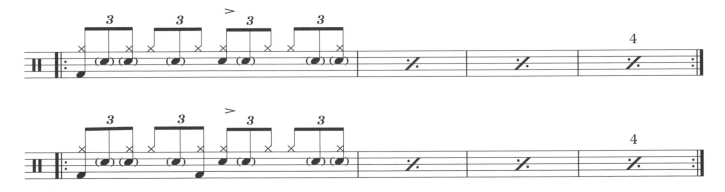

Chapter 5: Mangambe

Now we introduce our first African element: mangambe, or mangambeu as it's written in French. Mangambe is a popular musical style of the Bangante people of Cameroon.

Here's a simple version of the mangambe rhythm.

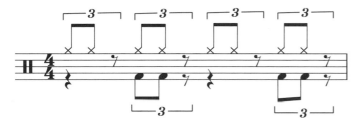

Here's a variation with the snare on beat 4. Notice the similarity between this rhythm and the American shuffle.

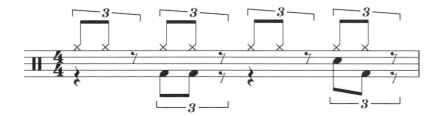

It's important to note that the notation above isn't a completely accurate representation of the sound and feel of the mangambe rhythm. First of all, the second partial of the triplet is emphasized. This accent is difficult for many Western drummers to hear, because Western music usually accents the first or third partial of the triplet, and rarely is the second partial emphasized.

In addition, the second partial is often delayed a bit, which causes it to exist in a space between the second partial and a straight 8th note. This interpretation can also be difficult for Westerners to hear, because it doesn't sit on a perfect triplet grid.

In the examples that follow, we combine the African mangambe with the American shuffle and the funk shuffle. How much you "Africanize" the rhythm and play outside the triplet grid should always be dictated by the musical situation. The music must always come first.

First, let's combine the mangambe hi-hat pattern with the American shuffle. As in the previous exercises, it's helpful to switch between four measures of a simple shuffle pattern, like the following, and the mangambe shuffles.

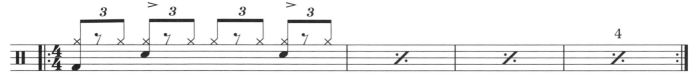

Here are the mangambe shuffle exercises.

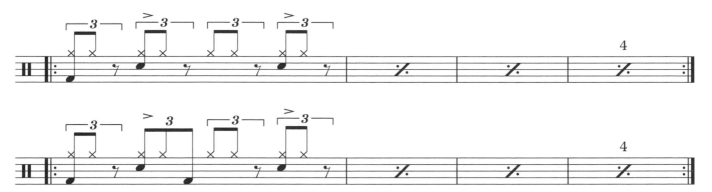

Here are the same exercises with ghost notes added on the snare.

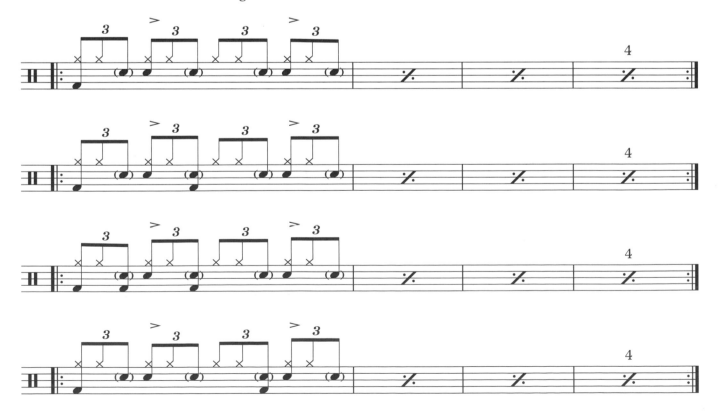

Next, combine the mangambe hi-hat pattern with the shuffle-funk groove.

Here are the same exercises with ghost notes added.

When you feel comfortable playing the previous exercises, move the hi-hat pattern to the ride cymbal and play quarter notes with the foot.

Another approach would be to fold some of the mangambe-style bass drum rhythms into the half-time funk groove, using the shuffle-funk hi-hat pattern.

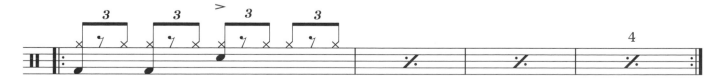

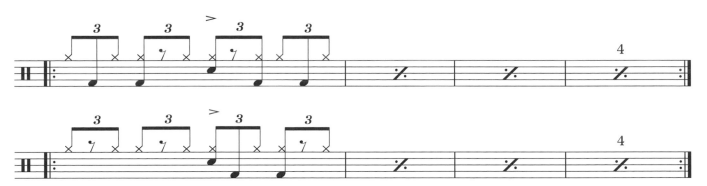

Now move the hi-hat pattern to the ride cymbal and play quarters on the hi-hat with the foot.

Next, move through the ghost-note patterns, gradually adding notes to make the groove denser.

Ghost Note Pattern 1

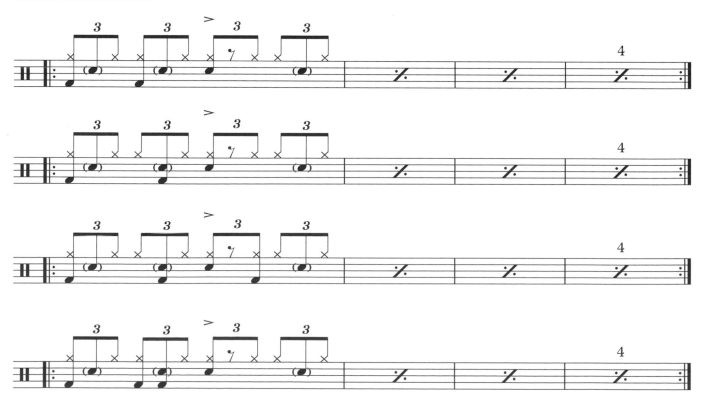

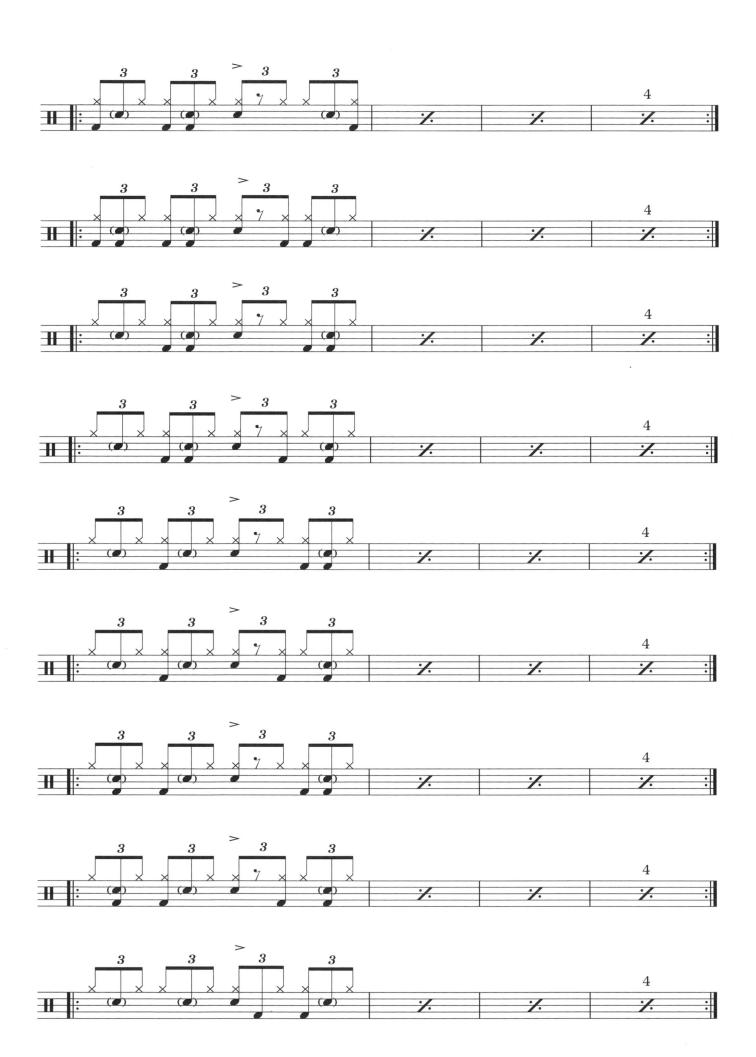

Ghost Note Pattern 1 With Ride Cymbal and Hi-Hat Foot

Ghost Note Pattern 2

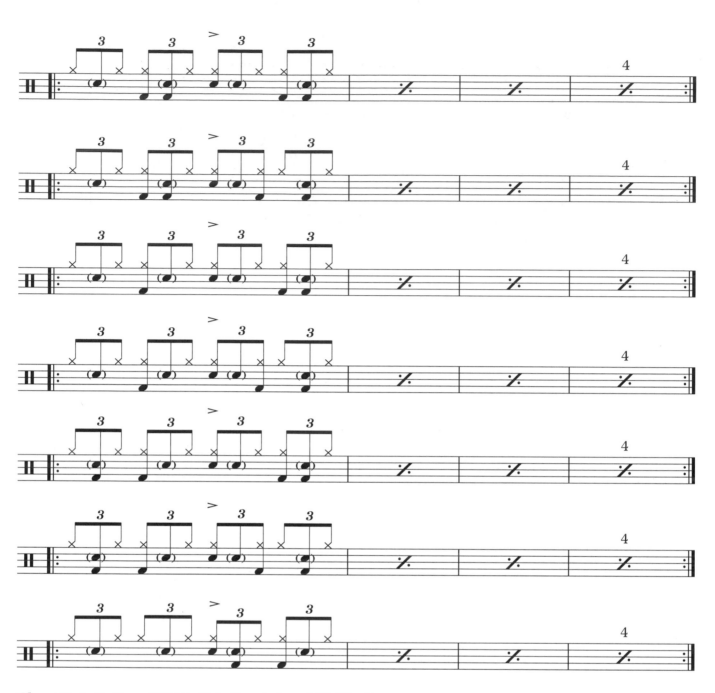

Ghost Note Pattern 2 With Ride Cymbal and Hi-Hat Foot

Ghost Note Pattern 3

Ghost Note Pattern 3 With Ride Cymbal and Hi-Hat Foot

Ghost Note Pattern 4

Ghost Note Pattern 4 With Ride Cymbal and Hi-Hat Foot

41

The final step is to play the mangambe hi-hat pattern over the mangambe bass drum patterns, while maintaining the shuffle-funk feel by accenting the snare on beat 3.

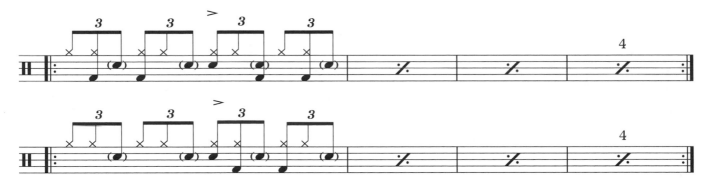

Now play the same rhythms, but move the hi-hat pattern to the ride and play quarter notes on the hi-hat with the foot.

Chapter 6: Bikutsi

In this chapter, we introduce the African rhythm known as bikutsi. Bikutsi is a musical genre from Cameroon that features the 3:4 polyrhythm. It has roots in the traditional music of the Beti people, who live around the city of Yaoundé, along with various elements of the pop-rock idiom.

The characteristic rhythm of the bikutsi is a grouping of triplets in a four-note pattern. Elements of this chapter are directly related to Chapters 1 and 2. If you aren't clear on the 3:4 polyrhythm, please review those chapters.

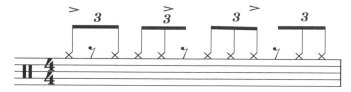

Here's an example of a bikutsi-pop drumset rhythm.

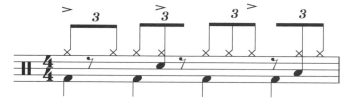

By moving the snare accent to beat 3, we can create a simple bikutsi shuffle-funk pattern.

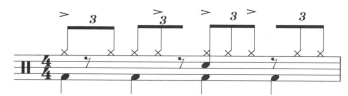

Here's a shuffle-funk variation with the bass drum on the first beat only.

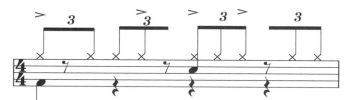

We can also open the hi-hat where the accents occur.

Here's the same variation with the bass drum on the first beat only.

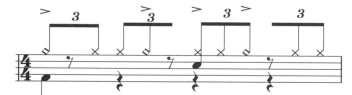

Here are the shuffle-funk bass drum patterns from the previous chapters with the bikutsi rhythm played on the hi-hat.

Next, move the hi-hat part to the ride cymbal and play quarter notes on the hi-hat with the foot. Here's a simple version.

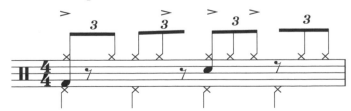

And here's the same variation with the shuffle-funk bass drum patterns added from the
previous exercises.

Here's a three-step process to create the long three on the hi-hat with the foot along with the bikutsi ride pattern.

Step 1: Play six against four on the hi-hat with the foot, which aligns with the accents that are played on the ride.

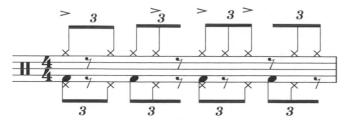

Step 2: Splash every other hi-hat note, starting on beat 1. These splashes can be achieved by using a heel-toe movement with the foot, creating the long three.

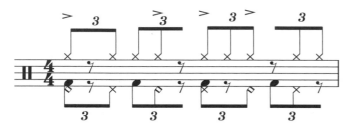

Step 3: Play the snare on beat 3.

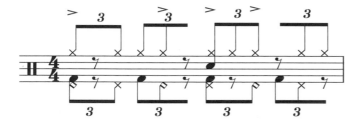

Here are the same patterns from before with the hi-hat splashing on every other note to create the long three.

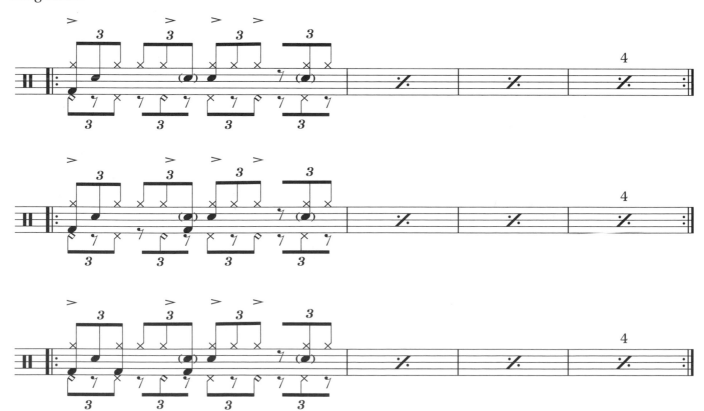

Chapter 7: African and American Combinations

The next step in our African-American journey is to combine the long-three polyrhythm in bikutsi with mangambe and shuffle-funk elements.

Let's begin by playing the mangambe right-hand pattern on the cymbal and the six-over-four polyrhythm with the foot on the hi-hat.

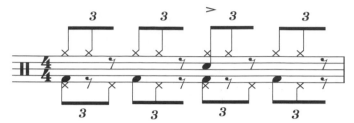

Next, splash the hi-hat on every other note to create the long-three feel.

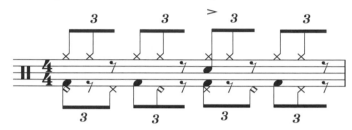

If you simplify the bass drum, you get a simpler shuffle-funk groove.

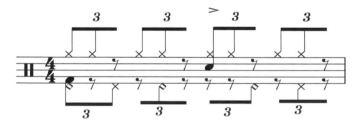

Here's the same groove with ghost notes added on the snare.

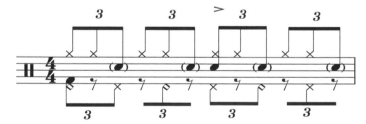

Here are the previous shuffle-funk bass drum patterns combined with the mangambe/bikutsi elements.

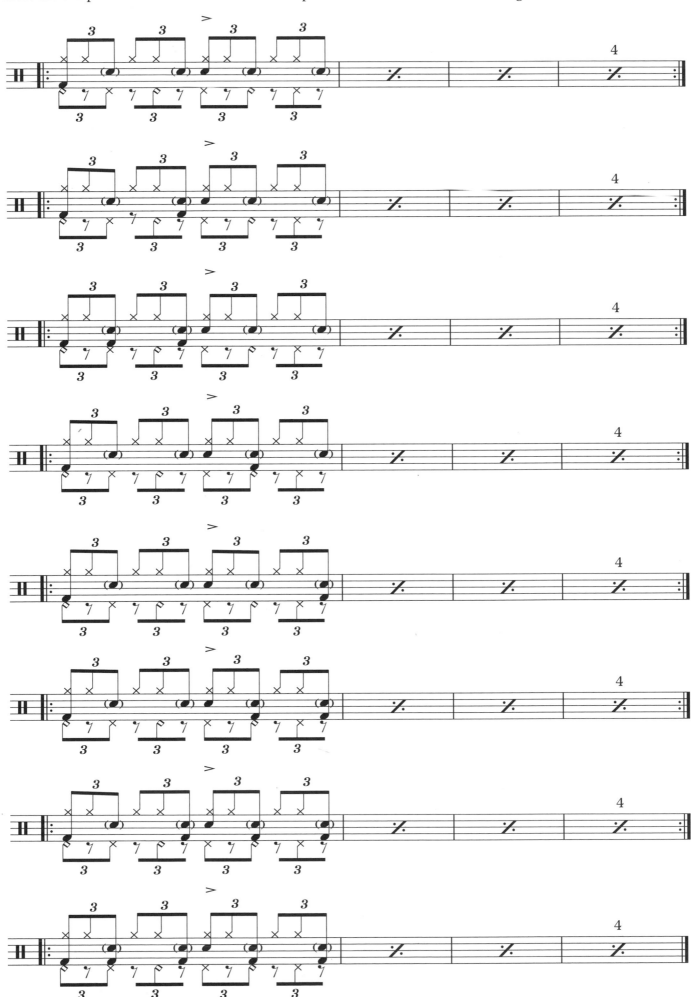

Finally, here are the same elements combined with the mangambe bass drum patterns.

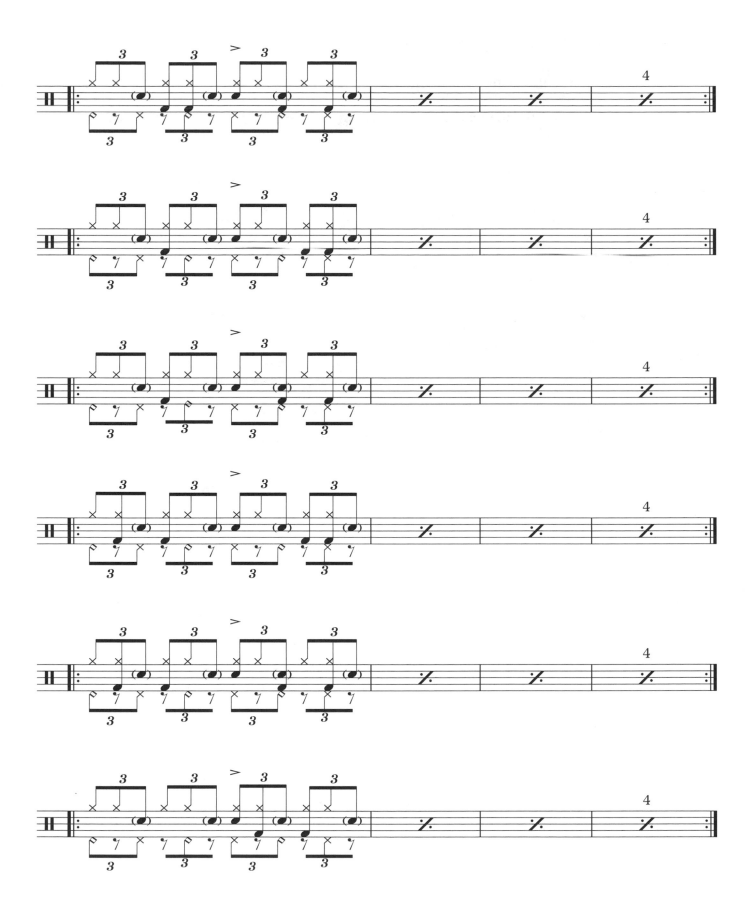

Chapter 8: African Pop Grooves

In this final chapter, we have some typical African pop grooves.

In the following exercises, the mangambe hi-hat patterns are used in measures 1 and 2, and the bikutsi hi-hat patterns are used in measures 3 and 4.

Now move the hi-hat part to the ride, and play quarter notes on the hi-hat with the foot.

In conclusion, we believe that the exercises contained in this book will greatly increase your rhythmic awareness and will open your ears to a new musical world. If you're at a loss for something to practice, or if you're in a rut, you might find this to be your go-to book for jump-starting your creativity and imagination. We sincerely hope that this material assists you in your development as a drummer and musician.